ADITI MACHADO

MATERIAL WITNESS

NIGHTBOAT BOOKS

NEW   YORK

T0282155

Printed in Lithuania

ISBN: 978-1-643-62244-6

Cover design and typesetting by Kit Schluter
Typeset in Gill Sans Nova and Horley Old Style

Cover Art: Adapted from "Portrait Sketch of a Costumed Lady"
by Paul Klee, 1924. Ink and graphite on paper,
Solomon R. Guggenheim Museum, New York,
Estate of Karl Nierendorf, by purchase.

Cataloging-in-publication data is available
from the Library of Congress

Nightboat Books
New York
www.nightboat.com

CONTENTS

MATERIAL WITNESS

It's Thursday. There's a band playing in the snow losing its distinction.
You film it, disaffected by the cold and the faces turning like leaves in a blue
    autumn.
The blizzard is a case of tinnitus.
A speculative wind blows through your instruments.
Coats fly open and blood boats.
The weather reports itself to a dead vertical left.
You film less out of sorrow than out of deference for the nonce of this music.
It is a balm.
It is a cold day full of plum deaths.

Yesterday was less cold. De facto blazing. You were visited by a pure
　　circumpapillary green that hurt your eyes.
Sometimes experience is phenomenal in its segues—do you remember you
　　were peeling a turnip.
That was some vegetable-colored sky toward which stupefied you grew.
You became its bespoke leek.
You were thinking something the climate kept controlling toward excess.
This is what it is like, you thought, listening to the assignations of trees.
Meanwhile you would not eat the turnip.
Meanwhile you sat on a tuffet.
Meanwhile you earned a degree handed to you from a helicopter in the sky.

Then there was the day before that and the day before that and on and on, concatenating your sense of being absent design.

There was the day you were sent a tube you presumed for breathing.

Had you bought it? Nigh impossible remembering anything resembling
   intention.

You held it, gentian, sort of frilled at one end, fluty at the other.

You put it to your face. You opened a bottle of acetone making a positive
   local escape.

Meaning you discovered you were sovereign.
You began to govern yourself by modes of wit.

You went to the beach and made to it an invertebrate overture.

You lay down, slug-like, slit-belly, what gave.

You were entering what then was called the universal. A bit pendulous.

You felt a motion that wasn't negative pulling you toward the ancient texts
    you had found floating in some sewage.

They were from the heyday of psychology.

You laughed at this.

An animal filament flickered at the edge of sea.

By sea they had meant mind.

You laughed at this.

You observed frothing something. Of the universe, what stung your toes.

Something universal at the edge you nipped into what you'd become.

Then came night at a slant and slit your mineral bosom.
Proverbial curtain except it sliced instead of fell clean through the fat of you,
doctor, nurse, patient, chaplain of time's bitter continuity.

Deaths, then.

And the foreshadowed room.

To your left and up on high: a talisman.

It radiated a summary of light.

It worked over you in a supervisory capacity.

Objects in your purview interrogated your semblance of shadow.

As it was in the first book: 'You had entered a poisoned room. The wills
  of things leapt out at you.'

Graphic you wrote.

At the nexus of weird speed and bird nest.

As it was in the second book: 'You lost perspective.'

The windowsill burst because it was too close.

Day of rebellion by means of suicide.
Day of rebellion by means of survival.

Then in matters of taste you became sensible.

Rare bottles brought up from the cellar dug up your nondominant tongue
for which there was a map inscribed on a low patch of kitchen wall,
chipped paint pointing to its location in bad faith.

This was a period of decay. No.

This was when you forked out opinion.

Your cruelty, uniform.

Caked in it, you wrote a definition against how it was yesterday.

Could it be you were divided into a body, politic?

Could it be you'd assumed governance, subjection, rebellion, pastoral care,
agrarian rites…

You released obscenity as from the fibrous heart of artichoke a quill.

Emergent wines, dated wines, you drank them all.

You could not, you would not, be touched.

Deaths, then. A green bath to strip out of, feeling yourself nothing in the dark but an orange erupts in odorous flame and kisses you with the kiss of its mouth.

You woke and were haunted.

Haunted by discursive strategy.

Haunted by an inability to name species.

'Hopping creature prone to dissembling.'

'Podded blue fluff.'

'Thornish venous luster.'

Your adjectival savvy versus an anfractuous trailing green.

You could solve this problem, in theory.

It would manifest in lowgrade sunshine.

Resting on a leafy matrix, your breath rushed into the ruins of some vegetal
   bones, the feeling of which eroded you, o student, o student of fortune…

Then there was no motion.

Then it picked up again, the 'always already etcetera' rejects.

Your stamina of compost.

It was like things deferred their freedom to you. No.

It was their kinetic enchantments.

Haunted in an old mining town turning private investment.

Haunted in its distinct odor of data, the labored sound of its pipes.

In the absence of culture. In the reduction and juice of it. You spat on the inklings of flowers.

Death to suburbia and you began to think again, militantly aroused resident alien of every which nowhere.

There was a radical in your gut. It measured the foreclosure of history.

You herded yourself into the killer mass. You became an agent. An agent of frottage.

Advertisements revealed to you the indelicate names of their products.

One day you dropped your valise and took a survey. The options pacified you, your biochemical responses a kind of legalese.

Once it had been written 'Sacred means saturated with being,' you spoke
that zone into obliteration, lying out of an abundance of caution in
untimely grasses.

You could have had visions, you could have had anything you wanted by
methods of indiscretion increasingly purveyed in those final years in
which lyric was put before all, lyric tea, lyric grant, lyric mass shooter,
give yourself up

except you couldn't, not to the accountants, not to the heightened
scrutability of the land, heights you'd fall off of.

Then an opaque zone. Or darkness bled. Impossible to extract confessions
when they're spilling already everywhere.

Then bloodless darkness. Dissent.

Trust nothing. The sun is president.

'Twas the modern death of history.
'Twas a heavy period.
Big chunks. Thick chunks. In your hair.
You restructured some lingonberries.
Into pie. Slip of the tongue.
Into particulate wetness.
Day of observance.
Day of war and bombing.
Day of gazing into the collective navel
and the progressive degenerative
lace of thine eye. What lurked behind
your antique set of taboos made the day
go idly by. No.

WHAT USE

To supplant the septum
ring, it is rousing,

it is a formal concern,
it is to raise it to lips,

the fruit entering its
ample folds, folds that augur

the present and to be here
now, wherein it creeps

out of you, what answers
you, in the violet unknown,

the period accelerating
into the eye like a gelatin

bullet, like surrogate
glitter, shreds of intensity

like light against needles
of the eastern hemlock

shreds, it is to go on
like this, to be repeatedly

denied, it is what it is
to be a formal concern,

and the feeling transcripts
making a little heap,

it is as it were,
down to the wire.

BENT RECORD

IN STARLIGHT and in the hum of typing I admit it was I.

I admit it was I who erased the posters in the mean street and

it was I who 'found' the body. It was I

who 'discovered' the plant and I who named it imperially

after my own self. Then I ironed out the language and I

showed my work in the cruddy journals of the time.

It is not the case that wax had dripped upon the pillow;

this was not the sign. But it is that I invested public moneys

in a variant distance off the shore in which the lighthouse

seemed a tallow stick. I did indeed compose the philosophy

and did so in broad daylight, bearing its illegible whips.

In this way I aroused complexity in myriad roses—*oh!*

pity the wild geranium and the dense

blazing star... But to return to that night, indeed it was I who witnessed the overwhelming meat and precedence

of summer as it received one into a vexed relation

with the cooling effects of trees. It was I who circulated

the yellow memo and I who poisoned the well. And I established

the literature, knowing full well the problems of the real world

to a less real one exquisitely apply. It was thus I of whom it was said

she availed of little caution. I came to surmise on the porch of autumn

with citrus discs and beads of solar attrition. I was akimbo,

I was inclined to fly. A flicker of madness. I had achieved

my historic high. And I knew just enough

to be toxic to the earth. In the raw bar of moonlight

I projected my one feeling which littered the street and mobilized

dawn and the sun came down its high metaphor and distended

the body's odor and it was I who said something is rotten

in the state… *for in such palaces as these one is armed with barbs to the teeth…* And yes,

I darkened the web and I defrauded the

publican and on stormy nights I withheld from classification

those very secrets which pierce the hearts of young historians.

Indeed it was I to whom it was said SLOW. THE. FUCK. DOWN.

And I did not.

I lived in directionless desire. Intransigent. Bullish. I ventured out

in viral fields. And I rode my bad scooter which killed the coral reef.

I withdrew my affections which bolstered certain militias.

And I suffered publicly excesses of feeling

which eliminated the most well-bred of my rivals.

It was under these circumstances that I came to speak for

the republic. And this is in the hot sun which burned to a cinder

the very thing I sought to make you forget and forget

you have, drinking the choicest of my ales. And yet

I have done only some of what I could do to secure my freedom.

Of nuance I am the consequent animal. Unsubtle,

I live in intricacies of the obvious. Into which I permit

your entry. For indeed, yes, over this too

I maintain a modicum of power.

CONCERNING MATTERS CULINARY

THAT EVERYTHING APPEAR
IN INFINITEST CLARITY

AND THAT MY TASTE
BE SUBJECT

    *

THE COLD INN
THIS DRESSING WARMS
AND THE SCALLIONS
WITHER IN MY ARMS

    *

THE TUNA SEARED
A BIT UNEVEN
SITS CADMIUM
UPON FINE SHEETS
OF GUAVA

    *

A LEAF OF CURRY
A SCENT OF LIME
EVADES DETECTION

*

PORTLY GRAPES
   THIS ASIDE

   *

ALWAYS THE VINAIGRETTES MEDIATE

   *

IS THIS NOT
MEDITATIVE

   *

SUCH LIPS PEELING BACK
THE ELEMENTS

AND THE SCALLIONS THAT
WITHER IN MY ARMS

   *

SO THAT I MEASURE
THIS ADVENTURE

SO THAT
I FERMENT

APPLES SICKEN

*

IN ONE PLACE THE FIG
ROLLS OVER AND
I STEM THE TIDE

*

FOR THIS AND ALL
THE WILD ONIONS
THE TERRIBLE EXCURSIONS
SUPPLY

*

DERELICT KOHLRABI
RIBBONS ON A
SHALLOW PLATE

BRIEF INTERLUDES
OF TENDER COCONUT
ROUND OUT THE SALAD

SALTED JUNIPER BERRIES
EYE THE MILD WHITE PEAKS
HAVING INTO A VALLEY DROPPED
FROM TREMORS

*

TENDER SCENT OF LIME

*

BECAUSE BASIL WILL NOT YIELD
TO FLESH
HORSES TAKE TO STREETS

THE BRIGHT BURNS ON THIS
LETTUCE RECALL

SOMEONE HERBACEOUS
SOMEONE SEVERED

*

SO
  MEMORY

*

SO BATED
THE SOLILOQUY

SO BURNT
THE BUCCAL CLAM

*

TWO ELEMENTS

THE TRIFLING BEEF
SET UPON
A CAULIFLOWER PUREE

THE INEFFABLE CURRY LEAF
INFUSING IT
REFUSES THIS
APPROPRIATION

*

SO I THOUGHT
I WAS WITNESS

TO SOMETHING
WITHIN ME

WHEN THE PLATTER
ARRIVED

WITH ITS FISH AND
CRAB AND TAMARIND

FLOWER DRIPPING
JUICES OCEANIC

*

ARRIVED
SET IN CURD
A CANDIED
GOOSEBERRY

*

ARRIVED
IN A GEL
THE GLOSSED
   EYES
OF A FISH

*

ARRIVED
THE PECULIAR FEELING
MY THOUGHTS WERE
INFUSING THE FOOD

INSTEAD OF THE OTHER
WAY AROUND

*

WAS THIS NOT MEDITATIVE

*

THAT I CHURNED
AND PUT THE CAT AWAY

*

THAT I SAVORED EVERY BITE
AND NEVER SPAT NOTHING OUT
THOUGH THERE WERE AT TIMES
ITEMS TOO CRUDE UPON THE PALATE
AND SEVERAL MONOTONE
OR BURNT

*

AND THE SCALLIONS THAT WITHER IN MY ARMS

*

WERE THOSE NOT MY LIPS
SACCHARINE LEFT DUMB
TO YOURS O PEACH MOUTH
IN WHICH I MACERATE

*

I'M FULL OF VICE
THE ERSTWHILE PIG
CRACKLES

*

WHAT SORT OF CORRIDOR
INTO THE SOUL
IS A KNIFE TO THE BELLY

*

I GO CRAZY FOR LACK OF PRECISE INSTRUMENTS

*

BITTER BEET PAINT
BEAT FACE OF ANIMAL
PLUMS UNDERWENT THIS

*

INTERLUDE OF LIME

*

THERE IS DEATH FOLDED
IN MY MOUSSE TODAY

*

DO YES INDUCT
THE OLIVE
AND KEEP PLUMP
EVERY CURRANT

PICKLE SLAW
AND LUSH
YOUR ADVANCES

I'LL BE MY OWN
STILL FRUIT

*

LEFT ALONE WITH MY PUDDING
IMPOSSIBLE SWEETMEATS
PROLONG THE MOMENT

*

SEASONED THE WINE
MULLED THE PARADOX
NOW PERPLEXED SOLUTIONS
TRICKLE INTO MY CUP

*

WUTHERING ARMS

*

BREAD ERUPTS
IN THIS YEASTY SUN-
CHOKED DOMESTICITY

I'M FRITTERING IN
IT HAPPENS BY SOUR
DESIGN

*

SO THAT I FORGET
TO PRESERVE THE CITRUS
MUSHROOMS GROW
FROM THE PEAR'S WELT

*

LIFE WITHOUT SCALLIONS
A SAGA

*

A LEAF OF BANANA
HOW DISPLACED

I CONSIDER ITS RIDGES

*

SO THAT CONFUSION
IS PRIMORDIAL
VINAIGRETTES

*

34

IT IS NOT

I FIND I AM

SAYING

THAT I DON'T

LOVE YOU BUT

THESE RABBIT BRAINS

ARE SO DELICATELY

FLOATING ISLANDS

ON THIS MILK OF GOAT

THE TERRIBLE PASTORAL

GARNISH BUCKLING

UNDER

I'VE LIVED FOR THIS

AND YOU HAVE NOT

LET US PART

ADSCRIPTIO:

SO THAT I DO NOT
OBSESS

SO THAT I DO NOT
OBSESS OVER THE FIG

I PLACE IT ON A RIM
SO THAT I DO NOT

FORGET THE FIG

I MOVE IT
IT BURSTS

THE SAP OF FIGS
IS CRUEL THE WAY THEY ARE WRAPPED
IS CRUEL

THEY BURST

SO THAT I LEARN
KINDNESS

THE FIG
THE FIG

FEELING TRANSCRIPTS FROM THE OUTPOST

To step into it, time being
funnily sequenced or accruing

laterally: a botanic tyranny
is moss, is how listening

dithers at the drum and I
follow it out to the fence.

There is a system to regress
in November. What they elect,

I supplant in private
and orphic degradation.

The garden affronts luxury
as it does moderation.

I burrow for radicals
against a less provident future.

For matter is in discord
like the forked philosophy

of a leafy bract subtending
the last measled bloom

of which I am regent
and which I uphold

against everything's
nothing. No, not

just that but the site's sublime
demolition.

It's like I have a second mouth
to degust in sedition.

NOW

you knew & how did you
to come here

you could say the literal obscenely
from this last language

breeds this iris
which deepens

you came
& you knew to come tender

you will do the work

you will tend these last
but accurate lives

you've come to tender
cognate w/ yellow

the yellow of the iris
so yellow the dew drops in

you've understood some things
the radiopassive light drips into

the wills & the vestments
the vulvate ear & flagellate bean

the acrid bellies of pig
the pink of the treetop

in the liveried scene
in which you learn this

& this & this &

now you're in the middle of the thing
beset by its obvious & lush features

mysterious garment draped across a low tree
you sniff its bouquet, it is an odor that goes
beyond description

who left this here & what do you remember
of persons, your hand going against the surface
tension ferns & false nasturtiums as you bend

to pick an arrant briar, your whole leg as tho
a bending filament, creepy tendrils spurting thru
the accursed growth of thyself

there are some prehistoric truths here
but where

now you take the train

you put on the hat & you drive the train

your hair pulses telegraphically

you have put on the exoskeleton of impure delight

pedicels fill upward into those umbels you call eyes

you drive to give the train its practice

you oil it, you move it in its happy ruin

you do this not for you—no, no

you do it for the bytheway foxes & the bytheway grasses, the bytheway
inured to these the metals of their collective conscious

it is for them you collect the movements, for them you fill the umbels

& like so the train makes its rosaceous entry into the boom boom patch
of nicotine grass

from between your quick & your nail
you extract a dark matter you roll into
a sphere, thereby inventing a black
berry named it-is-not-permitted-to-be-
bored

but this is life in the provinces
now that you afford pleasure

but you miss the freshness of eggs
you miss elliptical clarities, as in tulips
& your spineliness prevents a perfect
acquisition of repose

how can you sleep when it is so

when you wake disorder
of the bird kind hits the canopy
of a near dead tree & whatever other
senses are also hit

lawless you twitter
here ovum ovum here ovum ovum
you call to the missing

today the wind leans on your petals
& the sun flies over your sticky parts

today all the libraries are open to their custodian
which art thou

so noon the shadows of things get concentrated inside the things

so hot, your shadow

you tilt, imbalanced

there is gray matter at your feet

you absorb this puddle

something radiates out your molten core

you resent concepts that are past

but eject them, you cannot

the way you are dated

the way your eye tends to abstract from particulars shapes you deem platonic

the tendency of those shapes to hover above the particulars, doubling vision

your excess keratin belabors being

you try, you fail, the reason is optics

the optics are a bitch

the red road heads into a red mountain

you listen to snow melt at the horizon

red asphalt picks up the pink of olden reeds

you listen to dried-up pipelines

red dust stepping up to audition

in full-screen mode, the snow-tipped yarrow

censors your aesthetic, you cathect

a windmill in dry superabundance

cozying up to the cactus syndicate

you audit sonic fashions

you & your echinopsis bloom sillily

at this kinked-up altar of vocables

in this way lacerated

in this way salvific

the sounds of the desert tether you

to rusty pipelines shot thru

w/ hazard, heckling your sad little

human performance

now you speak, it's been
a minute, you open your
aaaaooooooeeeeee
you double your eff
ort, you keep, you keep
you repress an egress
your internal cactus
takes on a tinge, you
keep reshaping a
pore you keep open
you want to say, you
want to say but maybe
another day, you keep
your rictus

the secret of the mill is

you work it for your pleasure

& your pleasure takes the form

of its powdery white issue

drenched in flour

drenched in granular fission

you do you

& you just

you just bottle it

at the borders of systems always something a bit extra

like beyond the slash of begonia an ancillary, almost

bitter, pink—you linger there, drugged out

on phenotypical essences, craven & horny & hardwired

for whatever's on the brink splintering

mint serrated on the knife edge—you linger

by the exquisite corpse of this delay

dragged out & fatally nervous

& in the head derision roses

you minister the margins

of apoplectic reed, murmurs in the hearts of palms

a speed of thought hitherto unrealized

a speed of access to what's now

where the margin of error is is

out of an abundance of caution, you
outlast us, last humus

the cacti cum inside themselves—check

the sourdough mothers are rising—check

you enter the decommissioned tank & you light the candle—check

you look up & the pink dove—check

the pink dove is an emissary of pink

the mallow ears are filthy

you enter & you feed

the smokestacks

the smokestacks diffuse

oils of eucalypti

it is a eulogy—check

today's the switching on of lamps

the lamps of computers buzz about you

you till the soil, you interlope, the worm

in your arm breathes, it is the green vein of life

returning to its central location

your hand in the earth grows more

at times
you enter
a scler
otic zone
a solar
thing
pierces
the eye
you blink
as a matter
of policy
you sit with
the cryptic
you index
what you did
not sign
up for
a halo
on the in
fernal
division
of fact &
fury burns
you 'be
come'
silent

every sing
le thing
sends you
feedback

you pose continually
the question of your fertility

you have your menses
you have carnal knowledge

of ferns upon whom
you empty your bladder

it's a warning
it's a siren

vacuous sorrow
you must defeat

inner time rises to meet the peach
you place your lips against

green rays shoot out

it's only a pain & pain's a
direction dislocatedly pointing to
what's pleasure & when

& where are you, pacific infant
this isn't heart land

atonic trees released from their protocols
nevertheless shelter you & your

continental drift

a relation develops between the wind &
you that's lichenous, you who art green
to love, abstruse movements
brushing your burrs & birds, sine
qua non

sometimes it is a burden
to be so regardful, so cultishly
advertent of kingdoms that prosper
while you, o specious you, you putter
in your vehicular language
you suppress your vatic impulse

namely, you stand with your legs apart
namely, you odden into being

& an ill wind grates on
your chinny chin chin

now you take a boat, the boat makes a dissection, you reckon

water computes desire, that everyday needleshine

the smell of paint wafts into non sense newly

from the hull, you have taken your instruction

the sick flash of noon hits your sudden boat & there's a glitch

in the way you see now as inland you move your prow

now what fills you
is it light
how retro

now diabolical sages
now you pour into the coeval—there
where insects even will not
come, jezebel

now you enter an historical medium, it is called poppy field

you're in the middle of a red oil, you recall

some diseases take the form of love, you spread

by red contact, its neon amasses force against the hot blue sky

you're hit by vicissitudes of color you've bent against

severely, fire acquires

new angles by which to arrive at your back, you sweat

a layer of fat, texture you give to the middle distance

it is you who are oil

you who make the color stick, you who occult

what is present, you ruin

or let express an historical eye, it is unclear

vision that you had

vision that you dreamed

you quit charging

to light's capital

now you take on the color of the dead

now you're ivory w/ deckle

where you co-sleep with grasses, the air balsamic

an entropic transcript patterned on songs beyond

your kind, it is thetic & encrypted

something will reset it, somehow

it is the gothic cutting of radicals

it is radish soup, the making and quiet

consumption of it, it is you climbing

into your reflexes as nearby aniseed flexes

its peculiar muscles, slow & yellow, slow &

lime, you fall into a vigil of the waters

spooling pathetically around & coming to a

brownish rest you recognize vaguely

as your feet, so you ration out, protect yourself

from too much experience, you leave, say ecstasy

to the open mouths of lilies, leave, say

corruptions of idiom, leave them to the day

rashly diffusing into a stream of pixels, let it

express itself

ACKNOWLEDGMENTS

"Material Witness"

Excerpts from this poem appeared, often in different versions and under various titles, in *The Baffler* (no. 65), *jubilat* (no. 39), *Lana Turner* (no. 16), *Poem-A-Day* at poets.org (Dec. 2020), and *The Volta* (no. 55). "Sacred means saturated with being" is a line from Mei-mei Berssenbrugge's *Hello, the Roses*.

"What Use"

This poem first appeared in *Annulet* (no. 8).

"Bent Record"

This poem first appeared in *Annulet* (no. 8). The phrase "intricacies of the obvious" was uttered by Dan Singer in conversation with me somewhere in Denver sometime in the years between 2013 and 2018. Months or years later, when I lived in St. Louis, I emailed to ask if I could use it in a poem and, kindly, he said yes.

"Concerning Matters Culinary"

This serial poem first appeared in the *Chicago Review* (vol. 63, no. 3/4) in 2020 and later was selected for the *Chicago Review 75th Anniversary Anthology* in 2022. The title of this poem comes from the alleged "first" cookbook *De re coquinaria* compiled in the first century CE and attributed to the Roman gourmand Apicius. Thank you to the Latin reading group at University of Denver, and especially to Donna Beth Ellard for the time, energy, and patience you put toward teaching us this language.

"Feeling Transcripts from the Outpost"

Thank you, G. E. Patterson, for inviting me to write this poem for the "Poems as Maps II" special feature in the January 2024 issue of *Places Journal*. The poem was composed partly in my yard and partly in the street heading downhill to Vine. The phrase "against a less provident future" comes from the November chapter in Merrill C. Gilfillan's *Moods of the Ohio Moons*.

"NOW"

Thank you, Isabel Sobral Campos and Rita Sobral Campos of Sputnik & Fizzle, for making a beautiful chapbook (*now*, 2022) out of a substantial chunk of this serial poem. Individual sections, often in variant form, have also appeared in *BOMB* (no. 160), *Copenhagen* (no. 2), *POETRY* (vol. 219, no. 6), and *Volt* (no. 25). The earliest notes toward "NOW" were recorded on a houseboat in Sausalito (thank you to the Varda Artists Residency) in December 2018, and later, in March 2019, during a long walk in the Berkeley Botanical Gardens while reading Friederike Mayröcker's *Scardanelli* as translated by Jonathan Larson.

The section that begins "the red road heads into a red mountain" was written in March 2022 in Colorado Springs during a week-long stay at the historic Heller Center. Thank you to C. J. Martin and Julia Drescher for your kind hospitality and your friendship over the years.

The phrase "the margin of error is is" in the section that begins "at the borders of systems" arrived during a collaborative writing exercise with Sage Bard Gilbert and Katie Burgert in a park in Denver in May 2017. Thank you for letting me re-use it in this poem.

"the pink dove" is Etel Adnan's (see *The Arab Apocalypse*).

In the section that begins "where you co-sleep with grasses," the phrase "patterned on songs beyond / your kind" alludes to Paul Celan's poem "Thread Suns" or "Threadsuns" which I've read in many translations, by John Felstiner, Michael Hamburger, Pierre Joris, and perhaps others.

An early draft of "NOW" was presented at the Poetry & Poetics Workshop at University of Chicago in November 2020. Thank you, Kirsten (Kai) Ihns, for the invitation and, with the other attendees of the workshop (Ashleigh Cassemere-Stanfield, Tomas Miriti Pacheco, Srikanth Reddy, Jennifer Scappettone, and Brett Swensen), for the generous conversation that helped me think through the writing of this text.

I'm grateful to the editors of all the publications in which these poems first appeared as well as to everyone who has supported my work via invitations, conversations (private), and commentary (public) in recent years. I'm loath to attempt a comprehensive list as I'm sure to forget someone, but a few people—not already named—I absolutely must shoutout are: Raluca Albu, Toby Altman, Zach Anderson, Mary Jo Bang, Sohini Basak, Dan Beachy-Quick, Cal Bedient, Anselm Berrigan, Julie Carr, Kathryn Crim, Mónica de la Torre, Elisa Gabbert, Katrine Øgaard Jensen, Fady Joudah, Joyelle McSweeney, Joel Minor, Sawako Nakayasu, Sara Nicholson, Nathaniel Rosenthalis, Selah Saterstrom, James Scales, Brandon Shimoda, Rebekah Smith, Sanchari Sur, Brian Teare, Divya Victor, and S. Yarberry. Jaswinder Bolina, Amaranth Borsuk, Don Mee Choi, Gillian Conoley, Graham Foust,

Forrest Gander, Johannes Göransson, Lee Yew Leong, Farid Matuk, Stephen Motika, Daniel Owen, Carl Phillips, Srikanth Reddy, and Cole Swensen have helped this "extraordinary alien" in ways I cannot properly describe. Thank you also to Rosmarie and Keith Waldrop for letting me visit with you in the summer of 2021 and for sending me off with such a lot of books. Rest in peace, Keith.

Thank you to my oldest friends in the world, Kanika Agrawal and Sumant Srivathsan, and to my family (François, Min, Sid, & Su) for everything. And for making Cincinnati feel like (one of my) home(s), thank you, Alecia Beymer, Megan Crawford, Elijah Guerra, and Michael Peterson.

Thank you to everyone at Nightboat Books but especially to Emily Bark Brown, Lindsey Boldt, Lina Bergamini, Kit Schluter, and Stephen Motika who worked closely on making this book happen.

ADITI MACHADO is a poet, translator, and essayist. Her second book of poems *Emporium* (2020) received the James Laughlin Award. Her other works include the poetry collection *Some Beheadings* (2017), a translation from the French of Farid Tali's *Prosopopoeia* (2016), several poetry chapbooks, and an essay pamphlet titled *The End* (2020). Machado's work appears in journals like *BOMB*, *Lana Turner*, *Volt*, *The Chicago Review*, *Western Humanities Review*, and *Jacket2*.

NIGHTBOAT BOOKS

Nightboat Books, a nonprofit organization, seeks to develop audiences for writers whose work resists convention and transcends boundaries. We publish books rich with poignancy, intelligence, and risk. Please visit nightboat.org to learn about our titles and how you can support our future publications.

The following individuals have supported the publication of this book. We thank them for their generosity and commitment to the mission of Nightboat Books:

Kazim Ali, Anonymous (5), Ava Avnisan, Jean C. Ballantyne, Bill Bruns, V. Shannon Clyne, The Estate of Ulla Dydo, Photios Giovanis, Amanda Greenberger, David Groff, Parag Rajendra Khandhar, Vandana Khanna, Shari Leinwand, Johanna Li, Elizabeth Madans, Martha Melvoin, Care Motika, Elizabeth Motika, The Leslie Scalapino – O Books Fund, Amy Scholder, Thomas Shardlow, Ira Silverberg, Benjamin Taylor, Jerrie Whitfield and Richard Motika, and Issam Zineh

This book is made possible, in part, by grants from the New York City Department of Cultural Affairs in partnership with the City Council, the National Endowment for the Arts, and the New York State Council on the Arts Literature Program.